GW00707851

HEAVE HO!

HEAVE HO!

The Little Green Book of
SEASICKNESS

Adlard Coles Nautical • London

Published by Adlard Coles Nautical
an imprint of A & C Black Publishers Ltd
36 Soho Square, London W1D 3QY
www.adlardcoles.com

First edition 2009

ISBN 978-1-4081-1112-3

The publishers acknowledge and thank Charles Mazel
for the use of the quotes and extracts he researched for the
original edition of this book, entitled *Heave Ho: My Little Green
Book of Seasickness* © Charles Mazel 1993.

A CIP catalogue record for this book is available
from the British Library.

This book is produced using paper that is made from wood grown in
managed, sustainable forests. It is natural, renewable and recyclable.
The logging and manufacturing processes conform to the
environmental regulations of the country of origin.

Typeset in 9.5/12pt Steinberg Modern
Printed and bound in China by
South China Printing Company Ltd

A peculiar
AFFLICTION

'If you can get there by land,
do not go by water.'

Chinese Proverb

*

'Perhaps no malady to which mankind
is subject is productive of so much real
suffering, with so low a percentage
of mortality, as the peculiar affliction
known as seasickness.'

Scientific American, 1912

*

'I never saw the use of the sea.'

Benjamin Disraeli

'A man who goes to sea for pleasure would go to hell for a pastime.'

Samuel Johnson

*

'A stout wooden wedge driven in at my right temple and out at my left, a floating deposit of lukewarm oil in my throat, and a compression of the bridge of my nose in a blunt pair of pincers, these are the personal sensations by which I know we are off.'

Charles Dickens, The Calais Night-Mail, 1861

'Providence, while granting me an intense love of the sea, unfortunately failed to provide me with an interior suitable for its enjoyment, and I was usually among the first to make my little offering to the deep.'

W J B Crealock, Vagabonding Under Sail, 1951

*

'I have been seasick, and sick of the sea.'

Lord Byron, in a letter to a friend, 1809

'I once met a literary gentleman, who, on a voyage across the Northern Atlantic, tried every means to make himself sea-sick, in order that he might get the benefit of the trip, and failed, and was utterly disappointed. He smoked strong cigars in great excess, exposed himself in every way, and sought eagerly the symptoms that most people dread and flee from.'

George M Beard,
A Practical Treatise on Sea-Sickness, 1880

*

'If we are completely baffled, then I suppose we must be humble and let the argument do with us what it will, like a sailor trampling over seasick passengers.'

Plato, Theatetus 191A,
4th Century BC (Cornford Translation, 1957)

*

'He had his brother Tiberius put to death
without warning . . . and drove his
father-in-law Silanus to end his life by
cutting his throat with a razor. His charge
against the latter was that Silanus had not
followed him when he put to sea in stormy
weather, but had remained behind in the
hope of taking possession of the city in case
he should be lost in the storm . . .
Now as a matter of fact, Silanus was subject
to seasickness and wished to avoid
the discomforts of the voyage . . . '

Suetonius, Life of Caligula, 2nd Century AD
(Rolfe Translation, 1914)

*

'I was so seasick it was only the hope
of dying that kept me alive.'

Old joke

*

'For the sea is as nonsensical a thing as any
going. It never knows what to do with itself.
It hasn't got no employment for its mind,
and is always in a state of vacancy.
Like them polar bears in the wild-beast
shows as is constantly a-nodding their
heads from side to side, it never
can be quiet. Which is entirely owing
to its uncommon stupidity.'

Charles Dickens, Martin Chuzzlewit, 1843

'If a person suffers much from seasickness,
let him weigh it heavily in the balance.
I speak from experience:
it is no trifling evil.'

Charles Darwin, Voyage of the Beagle, 1839

*

'Cicero, having taken refuge on
board ship, preferred to return to Gaëa
and submit to the envoy of Mark Antony
commissioned to slay him than undergo
the misery of sea-sickness.'

The Lancet, 1891

*

'But why this qualmish, whence this queasy
    mood?

Have I swill'd flagons? swallowed noisome
    food?

Drugs I abhor, nor have I lately fed

With foreign beaux, who cleanse their plates
    with bread;

Nor native boors, who pick – beyond belief –

Their tusks with forks, then stick them in
    their beef:

No mental loathings flat upon the brain,

No dire prognosis form a tribe insane,

Disease the fancy – yet – slow langours
    creep,

Contagion low'rs – chill dews the temples
    steep,

Man's proud pre-eminence expiring lies,
And the last lanquet – soon – too soon will
    rise.
Dear, rich repast, the call of Nature wait,
Let her conduct thee to the postern gate,
There unreprov'd and hid form vulgar eyes,
Indulge the luxury of parting sighs!
O! hand a vase – alas! alas! – too late –
Weep, weep controllers of the bed of state –
Some healing hand for pity hold my brows –
Seaphic pens, record spontaneous vows!
If once on shore – away – a sluice prevails,
The world is delug'd! – sponges, mops, and
    pails!'

Anonymous,
The Sea-Sick Minstrel or Maritime Sorrows,
London 1796

*

THEORIES
as to cause

'Females, though a little more inclined to be sick than men, are still very hardy at sea, and probably accommodate themselves more speedily and completely to the circumstances than the other sex. Generally speaking, they can be managed by a little attention, and a few words bordering on flattery.'

Robert Mudie,
The Emigrant's Pocket Companion, 1832

*

'Persons with pendulous and flaccid abdomens suffer as a rule more intensely from seasickness than others.'

Nunn, The Lancet, 1881

'The relatively immune to naupathia are:
those with high blood pressure, the feverish,
the deaf and dumb, tabetics [syphilitics],
rope walkers, acrobats, dancers, the insane,
and young children.'

Dr J Bohee, Physician-in-Chief of the Ile de France,
quoted in Toubib, Hygeia, 1937

*

'What of the poor man?
He hires his boat and gets just as sick as
the rich man who sails in his yacht.'

Horace, Epistles, Circa 20 BC

*

'Motion sickness is unique among all the illnesses that afflict man. In common with childbirth (which is not normally considered an illness), it can cause complete temporary incapacitation without any pathological basis and entirely by reflex mechanisms, though unlike childbirth it serves no obvious purpose at all.'

Glaser, Proceedings of the Royal Society of Medicine, 1959

*

*

'A certain lot of cod, after being kept and
handled in laboratory tanks all one summer,
were placed in a tank aboard a boat for
transportation in the autumn. They had all
been fed an hour or so before being put on
the boat. This handling produced no effect.
However, after the boat had been under way
for some time, all the feed they had eaten was
seen to be on the bottom of the tank.
Thus, even codfish, after being ashore for
some time, may become seasick when
an ocean voyage is undertaken.'

McKenzie, 'Codfish in Captivity',
Progress reports of the Atlantic Biological Station,
Halifax NS, 1935

*

'When Dr Hayden was going to take a trip abroad he sought to put his theory [that sodium nitrate cures seasickness] to the test, but none of the passanges on the trip going over the Atlantic accommodated him by becoming ill. On the return voyage, however, he had better luck.'

Science, 1928

*

'Americans of both sexes, who are far more nervous than the English, suffer more from sea-sickness than the English do.'

Dr J Bohec, Physician-in-Chief of the Ile De France, quoted in Toubib, Hygeia, 1937

*

'As we rolled I felt that my internal economy was doing the same. At one moment all the moveable contents of the body, liquid and solid, were thrown one way, towards the feet, as it were; the next, they were thrown with violence upwards, and on the diaphragm, on the liver. This latter organ is so imprisoned under the ribs, so bound that is cannot get out of the way. Tickled, pounded, in this manner, it gets angry, excited, stimulated, pours out bile into the intestines and stomach, which ought never to receive it, except during the process of digestion, and this occasions sickness and vomiting.

Dr J Henry Bennett, The Lancet, 1874

*

'The notion that seasickness is entirely due to a disturbance of vision by continual changes of place in objects is shaken by the fact that blind persons are as subject to the affliction as those who see.'

Anonymous, The Lancet, 1843

*

'The attack begins as a rule with yawning or sighing; sooner or later there is nausea; and the last straw is supplied by the smell of a cigar or the careless remark of a bystander.'

Bennett, British Medical Journal, 1928

*

'Many people have a genuine curiosity to know if they would be seasick in case they should take an ocean voyage. An easy way to put the matter to a test is to stand before the ordinary bureau mirror that turns in its frame, and let some one move it slowly and slightly at first, and gradually growing faster, while you look fixedly at your own reflection. If you feel no effect whatever from it, the chances are that you can stand an ordinary voyage without any qualm.'

Hoyt, Old Ocean's Ferry, 1900

*

*

'It is not during the storm, when mountain
waves lift the prow of the vessel now high
in the air, and now plunge it as though
it were steered from the ocean's bed,
that sea-sickness most prevails. It is the
chopping sea after the storm that conquers
the stomach of even the weather-worn
sea-farer . . . The unenviable notoriety of
the English Channel, as a region where the
stoutest knees tremble and the ruddiest faces
grown pale, arises not from any superiority
in the height of waves, but from their
unequal character.'

Stevens, Scribner's Monthly, 1883

*

'Seasickness is a direct result of muscular disappointment and nervous perplexities, arising from the unaccustomed efforts to regulate locomotion, respiration, and vision with respect to the novel and extremely unsettled state of things on a ship.'

Stevens, Scribner's Monthly, 1883

*

'The human nervous system still remains that of a self-propelled animal designed to move at foot-pace through an essentially two-dimensional environment under normal earth gravity.'

Reason & Brand, Motion Sickness, 1975

*

'Thinkers, brain-workers, women, and the sick and nervous, the fearful, and members of the Latin race, are more susceptible than young children, the very old and weak, deaf, drunk, blind, deaf mutes, and members of the Anglo-Saxon race who are more or less of a phlegmatic temperament. Babies, persons of high courage and in good physical condition, such as acrobats or athletes, are immune, or less affected, from seasickness. The same is true of newly acquainted lovers. I found them always too busy to be bothered with seasickness.'

Capt Victor Seidelhuber,
No More Seasickness, 1935

*

*

'Riders borne by human carriers in sedan
chairs or on litters can also experience
motion sickness, particularly when carried
in a stately procession by several bearers
striding in unison. At least one pontiff
in recent times is reputed to have been
nauseated by the motion of the papal sedan.'

Guidnard and McCauley,
'The Accelerative Stimulus for Motion Sickness',
in *Motion and Space Sickness,*
G H Crampton (ED), 1990

*

*

'Of all maladies, seasickness must have
the record both for the number of theories
as to cause and for the diversity of methods
of treatment. More remarkable are the facts
that most of the theories are right
– in part – and that all the treatments,
no mater how ridiculous they may seem,
work – sometimes.

Robert Toubib,
'Seasickness', *Hygeia*, 1937

*

PSYCHOLOGICAL
EFFECTS

'Many of the greatest minds of the world have been upon the ocean, but how few great thoughts have been conceived at sea. Men of the highest genius seem to be transformed as soon as they get at a distance from land in a rolling ship.'

George M'Beard,
MD, Practical Treatise on Seasickness, 1880

*

'The victim of the wretched malady was regarded with loathing by those of his fellow-passengers who were inclined to be sick themselves, and with contempt by the few who felt perfectly well.'

James Owen Hannay, Spillikins, 1926

*

'By some happy fortune I was not seasick.
That was a thing to be proud of. I had not
always escaped before. If there is one thing
in the world that will make a man peculiarly
and insufferably self-conceited, it is to have
his stomach behave itself, the first day at sea,
when nearly all his comrades are seasick.'

Mark Twain, The Innocents Abroad, 1869

*

*

'In nearly all the letters that I receive
from my scientific friends in Europe the
invitations to visit us in America are met with
the statement that nothing prevents them but
the dread of seasickness, of which they have
some mild suggestions crossing the channel.
Undoubtedly ten times as many Europeans
would visit this country as now do,
were it not for this fear.'

George M Beard,
A Practical Treatise on Sea-Sickness, 1880

*

'I saw a man once, a courageous talker, urging his crew to sail in threatening weather. At sea, with the storm raging, you would find him without a word to say, under his cloak, for anyone to trample on who chose to.'

Sophocles, Ajax, Circa 450 BC

*

'Marcus Cato said that he had never repented but three times in his whole life; once was when he paid a ship's fare to a place instead of walking.'

Plutarch, Circa 110 AD

'"What happened?" whispered Arthur
in considerable awe.
"We took off," said Slartibartfast.
Arthur lay in startled stillness on the
acceleration couch. He wasn't certain whether
he had just got space-sickness or religion.'

Douglas Adams, Life,
The Universe, and Everything, 1982

*

'Lucien Guitry, France's greatest tragedian
since Sully, obstinately declined all offers [to
come to America] because he was sure that if
he embarked he would be seasick and if he
was seasick he would die.'

Basil Woon, The Frantic Atlantic, 1927

*

'Many persons will tell you that it is
an excellent thing to be sea-sick, as you are
so much better for afterwards. If you are a
sufferer you will do well to accept their
statements as entirely correct, since you
are thereby consoled and soothed, and the
malady doesn't care what you think a
bout it, one way or the other.'

Thomas W Knox, How to Travel, 1897

*

'It is an old adage that there is nothing worse than the sea to confound a man, be he ever so strong.'

Homer, circa 800 BC

*

'One ov the best temporary cures for pride and affektashun that I hav ever seen tried is sea sickness; a man who want tew vomit never puts on airs.'

Henry Wheeler Shaw (1818 – 1885)
Ods and Ens

*

'On a Channel steamer some years ago,
a faker made a good living – until he was
arrested – by selling bread pills to
passengers, among whom was his wife,
always the first who got marvellously well.
Though these pills had no therapeutic
value, it is a remarkable fact that many
passengers actually felt quite well
shortly after taking them.

I have found with most people that
seasickness is mostly imagination.
If they are able to get it off their
minds, and do not think of it,
in most cases nothing happens.'

Capt Victor Seidelhuber,
No more Seasickness, 1935

*

'Caesar's cavalry found that their horses, worn out with the effects of recent seasickness, were reluctant to keep on the move in pursuit of the enemy.'

Bellum Africanum, 47 BC

*

'. . . from the two "booby-hatches" came the steady hum of a subterranean waling and weeping. That irresistible wrester, sea-sickness, had overthrown the stoutest of their number, and the women and children were embracing and sobbing in all the agonies of the poor emigrant's first storm at sea.'

Redburn, His First voyage, 1848

*

'I knew what was the matter with them. They were seasick. And I was glad of it. We all like to see people seasick when we are not, ourselves. Playing whist by the cabin lamps, when it is storming outside, is pleasant; walking the quarter-deck in the moonlight is pleasant; smoking in the breezy foretop is pleasant, when one is not afraid to go up there; but these are all feeble and commonplace compared with the joy of seeing people suffering the miseries of seasickness.'

Mark Twain, The Innocents Abroad, 1869

*

*

'Medical psychologists are familiar with dozens of ways in which patients associate the sea with their mother – in other words, the sea is a mother symbol. For our present purpose we need only refer to one of these associations – viz., the respiratory rise and fall of the mother's breast while the child is taking food. The rise and fall of a boat during a sea voyage tends to remind people of this forgotten situation in an unconscious way, and sea-sickness with its rejection of food is a mode of repressing this infantile memory.'

W H B Stoddart, The Lancet, 1924

*

*

'The sicknesse of the Sea, wherewith
such are troubled as first begin to goe to
Sea, is a matter very ordinary; and yet if
the nature thereof were unknowne to men,
we should take it for the pangs of death,
seeing how it afflicts and torments while
it doth last, by the casting of the stomacke,
paine of the head, and other troublesome
accidents. But in truth this sicknesse so
common and ordinary happens unto men
by the change of the ayre and Sea.

For although it be true that the motion of
the Ship helpes much . . . yet the proper and
naturall cause, is the ayre and the vapours
of the Sea, the which doth so weaken and
trouble the body and the stomacke, which
are not accustomed thereunto, that they are
wonderfully moved and changed . . .'

*Joseph Acosta, 1588, Recorded in Samuel Purchas,
Purchas His Pilgrimes, 1625*

*

'In some patients the mental effect is slight; in others there is a strong conviction that death is imminent, followed, as time goes on, by an unreasonable annoyance at its delay.'

Bennett, British Medical Journal, 1928

*

'This is one of the compensations of the sea-sick. The extraordinary humiliation which accompanies their sufferings is very good for their moral characters.'

James Owen Hannay, Spillikins, 1926

*

'As the ship and I tossed on a wave,
And my stomach had naught left to save.
I let out with a shout
"Twould be better, no doubt,
To be lying quite still in my grave."'

Charles Mazel

*

OPIUM
and other remedies

'During an attack of seasickness,
one remedy is as good as another if taken
with confidence.'

Dr Bennett, British Medical Journal, 1928

*

'At the first sympton that the boat is going
to roll, drink some saline effervescing drink,
or a pint of champage. Do not drink
any alcohol, except champagne.'

Basil Woon, The Frantic Atlantic, 1927

*

'Take a fish that has been found in the
stomach of another fish, cook it, season with
pepper, and eat it as you go on board.'

*Quoted by Dr G H Niewenglowski
in Scientific American Supplement, 1909*

'A storm at sea produced widespread sea-sickness, but at the first suspicion of real danger many victims lost all the despondency of sea-sickness in an ecstacy of hymn singing.'

Hill, British Medical Journal, 1936

*

'Drink absinthe on sea voyages to prevent nausea.'

Pliny the Elder, Circa 60 AD

'The great bane of the ocean voyage is seasickness. The infallible remedy for it is yet to be found. Its mysteries defy the doctors and delight the cranks. Let your friends know you are going abroad and you will be told of enough medicines to stock a hospital. The most opposite methods of diet will be advised, one man telling you to eat all you can, the next advising temporary starvation.'

Robert Luce, Going Abroad?, 1897

*

'The only cure for seasickness is to sit on the shady side of an old brick church in the country.'

Old saying

*

'George Bernard Shaw has a method
of his own for preventing seasickness,
according to a letter in The British Medical
Journal. By relaxing his muscles and allowing
his knees to sag, he slithers up and down
the deck of a rolling ship past rows of green-
faced passengers huddled in their deck chairs,
and never, so he says, feels the slightest
nausea. The only trouble with his remedy
seems to be that it makes the other
passengers feel worse just to look at him.'

The New York Times, 1936

*

'The yolks of two raw eggs with
an equal bulk of good brandy
well beaten together.
A teaspoonful every ten minutes.'

*Partsch, Seasickness: Practical Precepts for
Ocean Travelers, 1890*

*

'I remember a certaine Englishe-Man,
who, when he went to sea, carried a
Bagge of Saffron next to his Stomach,
that he might conceale it, and so escape
custome; And whereas he was won't to be
always exceeding sea-sick; At that time
he continued very well, and felt
no provocation to vomit.'

*Sir Francis Bacon,
Historia Vitae et Mortis, 1623*

*

'One of the circus performers who arrived
yesterday from Germany . . . was Goo-gu,
the human pendulum, from the region
of the Yangtze, who entertained the
passangers during the stormy weather with
his novel remedy for seasickness. When the
ship was rolling her gunwhales under the
chops of the Channel, Goo-gu staggered out
on to the upper deck and suspended himself
by his toes to one of the battens athwartships,
where he swung rhythmically to and fro
for fifteen minutes. Then he felt so much
better that he was able to eat pea soup,
fat bacon and greens for lunch.'

The New York Times, March 20, 1922

*

'The sea will not cause nausea
in anyone who has drunk a mixture
of wine beforehand.'

Medical Monks of Salerno,
Regimen Sanitas Salernitanum, 12th Century AD

*

'So that you will not become sick on a ship:
Grind fleabane and wormwood
together in olive oil and vinegar,
and rub on the nostrils frequently.'

Pseudo-Apuleius Platonicus,
Herbarius, 2nd Century AD

*

'Henry Sidgwick, English philosopher . . .
would choose a secluded corner of the deck
and there declaim poetry at the rolling seas in
a loud and expressive tone and with emphatic
gesticulation. Given the opportunity, he could
keep it up for a couple of hours. But the
ship's officers would request him to desist.
His behaviour frightened other passengers
into thinking him deranged.'

The New York Times, 1936

*

'Take a handful of green wheat or grass,
pound it, pour a little water on it, press out
the juice, and let the patient drink a spoonful
every 10 minutes.'

From an undated handwritten manuscript,
Mystic Seaport Museum

*

'Bicarbonate of soda in cold water, with three
drops of peppermint.'

Capt Victor Seidelhuber,
No More Seasickness, 1935

*

'In Shetland, a drink of water in which is
placed a stone found in the stomach of a cod,
will prevent seasickness.'

Encyclopedia of Superstitions,
Folklore and the Occult Sciences, 1903

*

'Albumen is the only real cure that
we have ever found in sea-sickness, for when
nothing else will remain in the stomach,
eggs, boiled as hard as possible, will!
There can be nothing, perhaps, more
indigestible in a healthy stomach than hard
boiled eggs, yet in a sea-sick stomach there
is no remedy we have ever found so potent.
Eat from two to four and try them.'

James Arlington Bennett, MD, LLD,
The Art of Swimming, From Which Both Sexes
May Learn to Swim and Float on the Water, and
Rules for All Kinds of Bathing, in the Preservation
of Health, and Cure of Diseases: with the
Management of Diet from Infancy to
Old Age, and a Valuable Remedy Against
Sea-Sickness, 1846

*

'If any palliative be given, it should be large doses of ammonia with opium.'

Stevens, The Lancet, 1838

*

'I remember that he tried hot roast pig and bottled ale as a cure for sea-sickness; and that he took these remedies (usually in bed) day after day, with astonishing perseverance. I may add, for the information of the curious, that they decidedly failed.'

Dickens, American Notes, 1842

*

'I think one of the best remedies is to drink a little salt water, and frequently a piece of salt pork on a string will effect a cure.'

John Masefield, The New York Times, 1936

'In Iceland, a turf from a graveyard
is thought to be a sure
preventative of seasickness.'

*Encyclopedia of Superstitions,
Folklore and the Occult Sciences, 1903*

*

'Recumbent position, eyes closed, and a pint
of beer, ale, or porter taken in six or eight
doses at ten-minute intervals'

*Partsch, Seasickness: Practical Precepts
for Ocean Travelers, 1890*

*

'Nor could they have avoided sickness by
drinking salt water (pure or mixed with wine)
some days previously; or by using quince,
lemonpeel, the juice of sourish pomegranates;
or by fasting a long time and covering
their bellies in paper'

Rabelais, Gargantua & Pantagruel, 1552
(Jacques Leclercq Translation, 1936)

*

*

'Another very successful remedy
followed by a select number of persons is to
begin drinking as soon as the bar is opened
and continue the treatment until you are
in a condition when such sickness as ensues
may be rightly attributed otherwise than
to the motion of the ship. It is a curious
but exact fact that very few confirmed
topers are troubled by seasickness.'

Basil Woon, The Frantic Atlantic, 1927

*

'He went out to sea purposely to make himself seasick, and when in that condition he had a colleague of his douche cold water in both his ears simultaneously . . . This produced a decided lessening of his seasickness. Unfortunately, for therapeutic purposes, the relief lasted only as long as the douching was kept up.'

Fortune, 1947

*

'In diseases of the internal ear a relative immunity to accidental disturbances might be expected, and, indeed persons with perforated drums, previously martyrs to sea-sickness have been freed by their disability.'

Bennett, British Medical Journal, 1928

*

'There was a young man from Ostend
Who vowed he'd hold out till the end
But when halfway over
From Calais to Dover
He did what he didn't intend'

Toaster's Handbook, 1916

*

*

'About 2pm as one of the sailors were slushing the mizzen mast 60 or 70 feet high he accidentally dropped the slush pot, nearly full of grease, weighing 6 or 8 lbs and hit Elizabeth square on her left thigh, inflicting a severe bruise which is very painful but I trust not very serious . . . Elizabeth had been quite seasick up to the time of the accident but the fright attending that seems to have entirely cured her.'

G G Pierce, Manuscript Journal, 1868, Mystic Seaport Museum

*

'It is found by experience that if the abdominal muscles can be kept in an almost continuous state of contraction, the tendency to sea-sickness is very much lessened.'

Dr Nunn, The Lancet, 1881

'Always go on deck if you able to do so, even if you are carried up by your friends or the stewards and deposited in your chair like an armful of wet clothing.'

T W Knox, How to Travel, 1887

*

'On a recent aquatic excursion I was, as usual, very sick. I tried brandy, soda-water, coffee, &c., without the slightest benefit.

A lady on board was using brandy and salt for some purpose which I did not inquire about, but by mistake she put the salt (a teaspoonful) into a wineglass about half full of vinegar. This I mistook for brandy, which was by its side, and swallowed. In a few minutes I was delighted to find the sickness much abated, and on taking a second dose was perfectly relieved.'

A Freshwater Sailor, The Lancet, 1842

*

'Long ago green midshipmen in the English navy had a rope's end applied to them to stir them up to their duties, and sea-sick men on board whaling vessels had buckets of salt water dashed over them.'

Charteris, The Lancet, 1894

*

'. . . a good massage at the base of the skull, close to the center of the brain nerves, is very effective. Another practice – take a sharp comb and comb the scalp for about ten minutes upon rising in the morning. Massaging, as well as the combing, should be performed, if possible, by another person.'

Capt Victor Seidelhuber,
No more Seasickness, 1935

'Some persons recommend a tight-fitting undergarment of strong silk, but in order to be of use, it must be altogether too close for comfort, and the wearer is quite likely to say that he considers it the greater of the evils.'

T W Knox, How to Travel, 1887

*

'Paracelsus (1493-1541) and his followers, and all the other alchemists, leave mysterious, complicated formulas based on salt, alcohol, and of course – drinkable gold.'

Pezzi, La Cura del mal di mare Attraverso I Tempi, Ann. Med. Navale Roma, 1951

*

'It has been stated, on the best authority, that proprietors of passenger steamers are not likely to look with favour on any proposal to prevent the passengers from being sick, for that in estimating the cost of carrying – across the Atlantic, for example – the fact that a certain proportion of them will be sick, and therefore without appetite for an average number of days during each passage is taken into account, and that were sea-sickness prevented or materially lessened, while the scale of fares remains the same, the profits of the proprietors would be reduced.'

Chapman,
Sea-sickness and How to Prevent It, 1868

*

'Patient to lie flat on the back, and fold
a towel soaked in water, as hot as can be
endured and as tightly as possible around the
heat, reheating the towel at intervals.'

E Wolf, Letter to Scientific American, 1907

*

'Everything that can be swallowed has been
claimed to cure motion sickness.'

British Medical Journal, Editorial, 1952

ETIQUETTE
and
GOOD PRACTICE

'My husband is peculiarly liable to seasickness, Captain,' remarked the concerned wife. 'Could you tell him what to do in case of an attack?'

'That won't be necessary, madam,' replied the Captain; 'he'll do it.'

Toaster's Handbook, 1916

*

'If this is your first voyage, and you are not quite certain about the potential behaviour of your stomach, a table near the door leading to the first hatchway is indicated, and it may be wise to practise between the table and the hatch a little before the ship gets beyond Rum Row, just to see if you can improve your time.'

Basil Woon, *The Frantic Atlantic*, 1927

*

'There once was a man from Nantucket
Who at sea always carried a bucket
When he was asked why
He replied with a sigh
"I never know when I'll upchuck it"'

Charles Mazel

*

*

'Not long ago, during the annual Around Long Island Race, one member of the boat's crew became horribly seasick, but since the boat was racing, his fellow sailors refused to do anything about it. The sufferer resorted to waving his credit cards at passing vessels, attempting to purchase alternative transportation to shore.

The crew of one boat that came within earshot rebuffed him, saying, "Sorry, we don't take American Express."'

A true story

*

'All day we have been pitching and rolling,
producing a visible and rather "thinning"
effect on our dinner table. I ate no supper,
not withstanding which precaution,
I was obliged to "cast up my accounts"
about half past nine.'

Journal of Charles White Watson,
1859, Mystic Seaport Museum

*

'I had mal de mer once, aboard a private
yacht. If somebody had killed me I would
have made him my sole heir.'

Milton Berle

*

'How I should like to make love,
if only for the fun of the thing just to
keep one's hand in; but alas! All the young
girls are sick, and I trust I need not tell
you that a love-sick girl is one thing,
and a seasick girl another. I like to have
my love returned, but not my dinner.'

Thomas Chandler Haliburton,
The Letter-Bag of the Great Western, 1840

*

*

'It is a curious fact but no-one is ever seasick when on land. At sea you come across plenty of people very bad indeed, whole boat loads of them, but I never met a man yet, on land, who had ever known it or what it was to be seasick. Where the thousands upon thousands of bad sailors that swarm in every ship hide themselves when they are on land is a mystery.'

Jerome K Jerome, Three Men in a Boat, 1889

*

'If you should be so foolish as to be seasick, you must remember never to admit it adterwards . . . a good alibi is the only really effective remedy for seasickness.'

Basil Woon, The Frantic Atlantic, 1927

*

'I have said nothing, thus far, of that class of passengers who are compelled every day to make a sacrifice to the fishes . . . Happily, I have never been numbered among that unfortunate class, and am therefore incompetent to describe all their sufferings.'

P T Barnum, New York Atlas, 1844

*

'And I'm never, never sick at sea.'
'What, never?'
'No, never!'
'What, never?'
'Well, hardly ever.'

Gilbert and Sullivan, HMS Pinafore, 1878

*

'Seasickness has its obvious disadvantages
but it is a wonderful training for sprinters.
I have seen old gentlemen with gout disdain
their crutches when the Urge came,
and make the rail in nothing flat.'

Basil Woon, The Frantic Atlantic, 1927

*

'Sea-sickness is a very unpleasant
but often a very beneficial occurrence,
and in many cases might with more
propriety be sought than avoided.
It may not unfrequently be regarded as
an excellent preliminary to a residence
at the watering place which is the
destination of the voyager.'

Anonymous, The Lancet, 1832

*

'. . . for all its ludicrous horrors
seasickness is by no means a dangerous
affliction, and the great majority of ocean
voyagers are benefited rather than harmed
by the complete rest and total abstinence
it enforces. People who are not seasick
almost invariably eat too much at sea.
The salt air makes their appetite
prodigious, the hospitable steam ship
company gives them plenty of opportunity
to nibble between meals, and the result

is that they consume, on the average, twice or thrice their normal quantity of food. The victim of mal-de-mer is protected from this imprudence. Instead of eating too much he abandons eating altogether. And for most human beings a few days' fast now and then is a mighty good thing.'

Dr Leonard Keene Hirschberg, AB MD, New York Times, 1912

*